THE BIG BOOK OF
COWBOYS

Written and Illustrated by SYDNEY E. FLETCHER

GROSSET & DUNLAP *Publishers*

NEW YORK

HORSES AND COW HORSES · Cow punching demands plenty of hard riding from the cowboy, and plenty of wind and stamina from the horse. But not all Western horses are cow horses. A roping horse is a pony trained especially to work with his rider as a team, roping calves for branding. A circle horse, picked for wind and endurance, is used to help the cowboy round up cattle on the range. This job calls for miles of hard riding, since some grazing ranges cover

thousands of acres of pasture land. A cutting horse is a fast, nimble-footed pony trained to separate the "beeves"—full-grown beef steers ready for marketing—from the main herd at a fall roundup. Intelligent, fast in short, quick dashes, a good cutter will follow whatever steer the cowboy spots, quickly drive it through the main herd to the outer edge and then into the holding herd. In short, a good cow horse is not only a cowboy's mount but also his partner.

Texas Cowboy of the Lone Star Republic
The first American herdsmen were the
Texas "cowhunters" of the 1830's, later
called "cowboys," because of their youth.

The Spanish Vaquero of Early California
The "cowboy" of Mexico is still known
as a *vaquero*, which is the original Spanish word meaning "herdsman."

RIDERS OF THE RANGE · Cattle ranching has changed since the days of the
wide-open ranges of the Old West, but cows are still raised for the same purpose—
to grow calves for sale, and to provide steers for beef. The job of today's cowboy
remains about the same as that of the old-timer, and his riding gear and working
tools have not been changed to any great extent. Besides punching cattle, breaking and training cow horses, roping and branding calves, the cowboy must keep

The Southwestern Cowpoke of Today
Still the best roper in the business. He earned his name by poking steers to their feet through the slats of a cattle car.

The Northwestern Buckaroo of Today
From *vaquero*, this name describes the West's top broncobusters. Horses were raised before cows, in the Northwest.

drift fences—the barbed-wire fences erected to keep cattle on their home range—in constant repair. In the spring, the cowboy must "ride bog" around water holes where, invariably, a number of cattle get bogged down in mud or quicksand. To free the cow (as the cowboy calls anything with four legs and horns, regardless of sex), he ropes it around the neck, and then, with his pony's help, drags the critter out onto solid ground.

RIDE 'EM, COWBOY! · Taming the "rough string," wild, unbroken horses, is accomplished by the outfit's top bronc rider, with other cowboys helping, and takes about six weeks. "Broke" covers a wide range of so-called tameness—even the trained cow horse may buck a few jumps every time he is mounted. The breaking corral, forty to fifty feet in diameter, is circled by an eight-foot fence of heavy wooden posts, to which rails are fastened by rawhide strips. Top rail

is the "opera house," grandstand seat for watching ranch hands. A cloth over the horse's eyes quiets him for saddling—then the fun begins. Large ranches hire a "contract buster," who, at a flat rate per head, will break a horse in a day's work. Such treatment, however, may break the horse's spirit, too. But some horses never accept the saddle. These are the "outlaws" you see in rodeos, fighting it out with the broncobusters.

B HEART	BRIDLE BIT
ARROWHEAD	RUNNING O
SWING EASY	BOX W
SNAKE IN MOON	HORSESHOE BAR
KENO	RAFTER DIAMOND
ROCKING R	CIRCLE DOT
COVERED STAR	2 TRIANGLE
BARBEQUE	RAIN BARREL
HOLE IN BOX	TUMBLING A BAR
ARROW E	SLASH TRIANGLE

THE IRON MAN · Since early Egyptian days, the burned-in brand has been important, to identify and protect livestock. Today, the working cattle, horse, and sheep brands registered in our Western range country run into hundreds of thousands. At spring roundup, cowboys rope and brand the newborn calves and

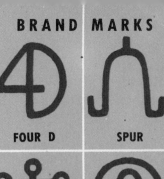

the yearlings — grown calves weaned from their mothers but not yet two years old. A two-year-old maverick (unbranded critter) is hard to find. The branding iron, heated until "cherry red," is held against the calf's flank for half a minute. It scorches the hair and leaves a scar but doesn't really hurt the calf.

FAN 'EM, COWBOY! · All cowboys, of course, must be good riders, but a top bronc rider is said to be born, not made. In a rodeo riding contest, the cowboy aims to ride the bucking horse for ten seconds without "grabbing leather"—that is, without touching the saddle with hat or hand. An outlaw horse can make those ten seconds feel like half an hour. Already infuriated by the "bucking strap" buckled tightly behind his ribs, he tries every low-down trick he knows to shake

the rider off his back. The cowboy, meanwhile, eggs him on even further, in order to demonstrate his riding skill to the judges. A mean bucker, with his mind on his work, generally can throw his rider on the first jump. If that doesn't do the trick, he has time for twenty or thirty more jumps that will practically guarantee it. And a broncobuster pitched off a tall horse falls a long distance, and discovers suddenly that the ground can be very, very hard indeed.

DOGGERS ON THE TRACK! · Another popular rodeo contest event is bull-dogging, or steer wrestling, in which the cowboy tries to stop a full-grown, running steer and throw him to the ground in the shortest possible time. The steer is held in the chute, a narrow passage with high walls, while the cowboy waits on his horse. When the chute gate flies open, the steer breaks out like a shot and the dogger takes after him at top speed. Reaching the bull's flanks, the

cowboy quits the saddle head first, grabs the bull's horns with both hands, digs in his heels, and sits down, pulling the steer's head sharply around. Then the dogger straddles the left horn, passes both arms behind the right horn, and grabs the bull by the nose, twisting it upward and walking backward. The bull is thrown off balance and down he goes, horns on the ground and his nose pointing sky-ward. A good dogger can wrestle a steer to the ground in seven seconds flat.

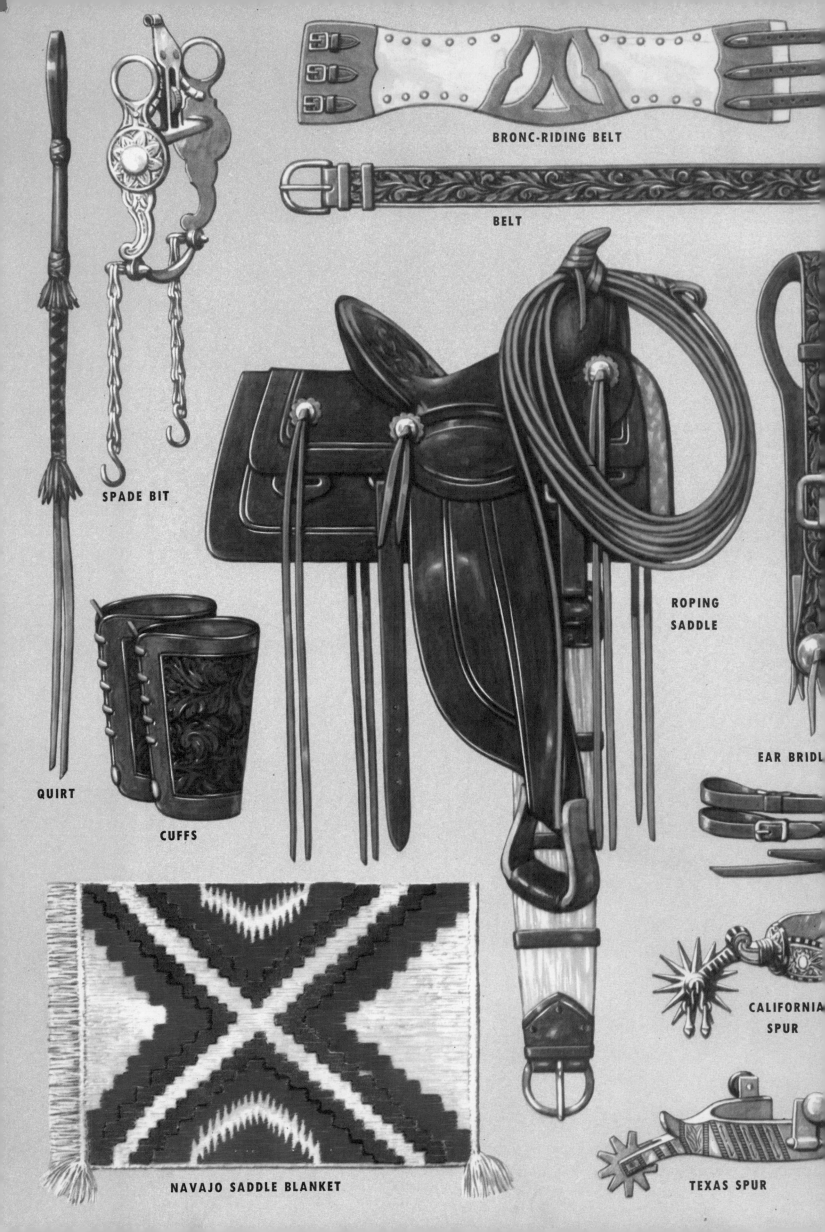

QUIRT

SPADE BIT

CUFFS

BRONC-RIDING BELT

BELT

ROPING SADDLE

EAR BRIDL

NAVAJO SADDLE BLANKET

CALIFORNIA SPUR

TEXAS SPUR

HORSE HOBBLES

COWBOY BOOTS

MUFFLER

ROPING GLOVES

SHOW VEST

ANGORA
SHOW CHAPS

BATWING
SHOW CHAPS

ULL BRIDLE

LIT REINS

R STRAPS

THE COWBOY'S RIDING
AND WORKING GEAR

*Descriptions of the various articles of
cowboy gear shown on these pages will
be found in the back of the book.*

HEADED FOR THE ROUNDUP · Busiest times for cowboys are the two annual roundups. In spring, newborn calves are branded. In the fall, cowboys ride out to the grazing ranges, taking extra mounts, called the *remuda* in the Southwest, the "saddle band" in the Northwest. From dawn to sundown, circle riders comb the ranges for cattle, drive them to where the main herd is assembling. Cutters then turn graded beeves into the holding herd. Beef cattle is classified according

to age and condition. A-1, best grade, is "prime" beef. If several ranches join forces in a "pool roundup," beeves are separated by their brand marks into different holding herds. In early days, to reach railroad loading points, cattle had to be driven overland on the hoof, along the famous Chisholm Trail in Texas, and other trails. Now, trailed across country in short drives, with time to graze and water, beef steers reach the cattle cars at the railroad siding in top condition.

COME AND GET IT! · A crew of hard-working range riders can consume a lot of grub in a month. The traveling kitchen of cattle ranchers on a roundup is the chuck wagon. Drawn by four mules and driven by the ranch cook, it is crammed with food, stew kettles, frying pans, Dutch ovens (shallow iron kettles for baking, with a rimmed cover to hold burning coals), and a giant, two-gallon coffeepot. In the rear is the cook's kitchen cabinet, a big box with a single door

that becomes a worktable when lowered onto a drop leg. Spare equipment and the crew's bedrolls are stowed in the front, protected in bad weather by a canvas cover stretched over wooden bows. Cowboy grub is wholesome, not fancy. Coffee sweetened with blackstrap (the original, unrefined molasses used for cooking), beans, salt side of pork or bacon, spuds, onions, dried fruit, canned goods—generally tomatoes—are the stand-bys. And, of course, there's always plenty of beef.

FORTY BELOW · Sudden blizzards from the north, that blow icy blasts of cutting sleet and blinding snow across the frozen cattle ranges, are the cowboy's greatest dread in winter. There is little he can do for the herd. What winter pasturage there is, is soon covered by a hard crust of snow and ice, through which the starving cattle cannot seem to penetrate. Unlike buffaloes, which hunch their shoulders into the wind and let the storm eventually blow past them, cattle caught in a

blizzard always drift before the wind, struggling along on fast-numbing legs, try-ing to keep from freezing to death. If a steer goes down in the snow, it is certain to perish. In fact, neither man nor beast can be sure of survival. But the cowboy bundles up as best he can against the bitter sub-zero cold, alternates with his part-ner in snatching temporary shelter in a little cabin on the range, watches his drift fences, and stays with the herd.

SING THE SONG OF THE HERD · Many early cowboy ballads were composed around a campfire and sung to the plaintive strains of some cowboy's harmonica. Songs like "The Chisholm Trail" and "I Ride an Old Paint" tell of longhorns, of trail drives, and stampedes. The lively rhythm matches the brisk beat of the pony's hoofs on the trail, for if the cowboy sang in one rhythm and his pony's gait beat out another, the rider would soon have his wind knocked

out. But the songs of the night herd, such as "Bury Me Not on the Lone Prairie" and "Barbara Allen," are slow, mournful tunes adapted to the ambling walk of the cow pony as he and his rider make their lonely rounds on herd guard, under the stars. These are the ballads the cowboy sings to the bedded-down cattle, to overcome night sounds that might frighten them. And though somewhat off key at times, the sound of the cowboy's singing seems to reassure and comfort the herd.

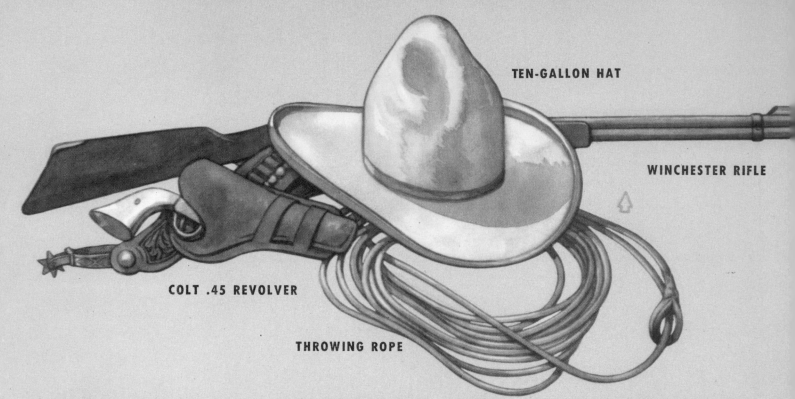

TEN-GALLON HAT

WINCHESTER RIFLE

COLT .45 REVOLVER

THROWING ROPE

A DICTIONARY OF COWBOY RIDING AND WORKING GEAR

ANGORA SHOW CHAPS. "Hair" pants worn on the Northwestern ranges in winter for warmth. Generally made of Angora white or black goatskin, sometimes of bearskin, those used for show purposes are often dyed bright colors.

BATWING SHOW CHAPS. Leather coverings, usually made of cowhide, worn to protect the cowboy's legs in riding through rough brush, such as the prickly pear cactus and chaparral of the Southwest. Chaps are strapped to the waist and closed around the leg with snaps, so that they can be taken off without removing the spurs. "Dress-up" batwings are decorated with brightly colored, appliquéd leather and silver or brass studs.

BELT. A cowboy's working blue denim overalls are tight fitting around the waist and need no belt. But he likes to wear a fancy, hand-carved leather belt on occasions.

BRONC-RIDING BELT. Used in bronc-riding contests, or in horse breaking, as a brace to strengthen the wall of the back against kidney injuries.

CALIFORNIA SPUR. The elaborate, hand-forged, silver-inlaid spur popular west of the Rockies. Beautifully made, it retains much of the spur design used by the early Spanish *caballeros,* or herdsmen, of California.

COLT .45 REVOLVER. The six-gun invented by Samuel Colt, and used throughout the cow country. One of the early models was nicknamed "The Peacemaker," because of the part it played in bringing law and order to the old frontier.

COWBOY BOOTS. Finest footgear ever devised for the horseman, the high heel prevents the foot from being caught in the stirrup if the rider is thrown. The reinforced arch is less tiring, as it supports the rider's weight well. The shaped toe finds the stirrups quickly in mounting. Fancy designs on the tops are added by the bootmakers to catch the eye. Pee-wees (boots worn by bronc riders) have tight-fitting, strong tops to save the ankles from strain.

CUFFS. Worn to protect the wrists and prevent rope burns. (See ROPING GLOVES.)

EAR BRIDLE. A simple type of headstall, held in place by passing the horse's ear (usually the left one) through a slit in the crown piece. Some are made with slits for both ears.

FULL BRIDLE. More elaborate than the ear bridle, this has a brow band, sometimes a nose band, and a throat latch which passes around the horse's neck. The bit is tied to both types of bridles by rawhide thongs attached to the ends of the check pieces.

HORNSPREAD OF TEXAS LONGHORN. The old-time steer had a spread of horn ranging from four to six feet, from tip to tip. Grazing at will over the open range, these steers were half-wild, tough, and weighed from eight hundred to a thousand pounds.

HORSE HOBBLES. Strapped around the forelegs, they permit a horse to graze at will, at the same time preventing him from wandering off very far.

MUFFLER. The handkerchief the cowboy ties loosely around his neck. He wipes the perspiration out of his eyes with his "neckpiece," then lets it go, to flutter in the breeze, which soon dries it.

NAVAJO SADDLE BLANKET. An Indian hand-woven woolen blanket, it is one of the best made, lying smoothly on the horse's back, absorbing sweat readily, and requiring no washing.

QUIRT. A handmade whip of braided rawhide.

ROPING GLOVES. Heavy buckskin or horsehide gloves worn to prevent the cowboy's hands from being burned by the "hot rope" being dragged through them by the steer on the other end.

ROPING SADDLE. Constructed differently from a bronc-riding saddle, it is primarily a work seat, with a strong, steel roping horn and a low, sloping cantle (rear projection of the saddle).

SHOW VEST. A carryall for the cowboy's "makings." The old-time cow hand used to say he wore a vest to keep from catching a cold.

SPADE BIT. A type of Western bit used to control a stubborn or mean horse.

SPLIT REINS. Separate reins, preferred by the Southwestern cowboy. In California and on the Northwestern ranges, reins generally are tied together, the long ends also serving as a quirt.

SPUR STRAPS. These pass over the instep and, together with the chain or strap passing under the arch, hold spurs to the boot heels.

TEN-GALLON HAT. The perfect headgear for outdoor work, it serves both as a sunshade and an umbrella. The cowboy calls it his "John B.," after the John B. Stetson Company, of Philadelphia, manufacturers of famous range-riding "sombreros."

TEXAS SPUR. A machine-forged, mass-produced spur, strong and simple in pattern, used by Southwestern cowpokes as a "grappling iron."

THROWING ROPE. Used in roping "cows," the length varies in different parts of the range country. The Texas cowboy uses a rope about forty feet long. West of the Rockies, a sixty-foot rope is preferred. Twenty-five to thirty feet is an average throw.

WINCHESTER RIFLE. Greeted with suspicion when it first appeared, the Winchester repeating rifle proved itself, and has been the cowboys' favorite saddle carbine ever since. It is sturdy, doesn't jam, and is remarkably accurate.

HORNSPREAD OF TEXAS LONGHORN